JAMES DE KOVEN
Anglican Saint

Edited by

Thomas C. Reeves

The DeKoven Foundation for Church Work
Racine, Wisconsin 53403

ISBN: 0-910494-03-7

© 1978 The DeKoven Foundation for Church Work
Racine, Wisconsin 53403
Printed in the United States of America

"Wisdom is a gift of God. Counsel, ghostly strength and knowledge, are graces of the Blessed Spirit. They must be given, in all their fullness and in all their power, to the purest heart and the most innocent life."

James De Koven

INTRODUCTION

WHEN JAMES DE KOVEN died unexpectedly in 1879 at the age of 47, a profound sense of tragedy overwhelmed those who had known him even slightly. As a priest, churchman, educator, preacher and writer he had influenced the lives of thousands, and was thought by some to be the major figure in the Protestant Episcopal Church. He was described by an intimate as "not only one of the most brilliant orators, one of the finest scholars, one of the most clear debaters in the Church, but he was one of the holiest, one of the saintliest of all her sons." In 1892 Frederic Cook Morehouse called him "the greatest product of the American Church during the century."

In our own time he has been nominated as the only saint produced by the Episcopal Church. The Assistant Dean of Seabury-Western seminary said in a sermon, "I have no hesitation in saying 'Blessed James de Koven, pray for us,' " In 1963 the Standing Liturgical Commission placed his name in the Church calendar, noting that he "has left a permanent stamp upon the learning and piety of the Episcopal Church, through his reasoned and compelling defense of its Catholic heritage . . . "

De Koven was born on September 19, 1831 in Middletown, Connecticut, the ninth of ten children. His father, a banker who died in 1840, was of German origin, while his mother could trace her English ancestry to John Winthrop. He grew up in Brooklyn Heights, New York and displayed intellectual prowess at an early age. At twelve he wrote an Epiphany hymn that was sung in at least one local church, and at fifteen he published a small book of poems. He graduated second in his class from Columbia College in 1851 and followed the path of an older brother into the service of the Church. In 1854 he graduated as valedictorian from General Theological Seminary and shortly thereafter was ordained to the diaconate. While a seminarian, he established a "ragged school" for underprivileged boys from the streets of New York. A classmate later recalled, "how lovingly did James De Koven work with those poor outcasts!"

General Theological Seminary was the national center of High Churchmanship, an emphasis upon the Catholicity of the Episcopal Church with roots in the teachings of American Bishops Samuel Seabury and John Henry Hobart and in the Church of England's Oxford Movement. De Koven emerged an advanced High Churchman, or ritualist, uncompromisingly committed to Catholic liturgy, ceremonial and architecture. His devotion to the sacraments, his desire to beautify church services with altar lights, incense, flowers, crosses, ornate vestments and the like, plus his missionary zeal, placed him throughout his lifetime within a minority of his priestly peers. Today, many of his beliefs about doctrine and ritual are commonplace in the Church.

De Koven declined offers from two prosperous East Coast parishes, choosing instead to accept the Chair of Ecclesiastical History at Nashotah House, a struggling little seminary, monastery and missionary center in the forests of Wisconsin west of Milwaukee. He also became rector of the Church of St. John Chrysostom in nearby Delafield. He was ordained to the priesthood at Delafield by the great missionary Bishop Jackson Kemper on September 23, 1855.

Three years later De Koven assumed yet another duty, becoming Warden of St. John's Hall, a new institution designed to prepare boys for Nashotah. A severe depression ravaging the country prompted a merger in 1859 between St. John's Hall and Racine College, an impoverished school on Lake Michigan that had opened in 1852 with nine students and a single professor.

At 28, De Koven became Warden of Racine College, and over the next two decades he devoted his extraordinary intellect and energy to the school, making it the most distinguished college college west of the Alleghenies. Buildings shot up, the number of faculty and students increased (at one point there were 220 students in the college and grammar school), and the quality of education reached a high level. In 1875 the Bishops of Michigan, Indiana, Nebraska, Missouri, Colorado, Wisconsin, Western Michigan, Illinois and Fond du Lac adopted Racine as the collegiate institution of their dioceses, vowing to make it a church university for the West and Northwest.

Racine College became widely known for its dedication to De Koven's High Church convictions. Chapel was held twice a day and evensong featured a vested choir of thirty-two students. On occasion, De Koven provided the Sacrament of Penance for the young men.

De Koven was deeply loved and respected by students, some coming from as far away as New York, San Francisco, and New Orleans to live, study and pray in his presence. He told them stories on Sunday afternoons (one was published as *The Dorchester Polytechnic Academy*, and still makes delightful reading), held receptions on Sunday evenings, and treated them to many displays of inspired oratory. The Rev. Morgan Dix of Trinity Church, New York, once said of De Koven's preaching:

> Who can convey an idea to one who never saw or heard him, of the effect produced by that impassioned manner and that wonderful voice, which, now ringing like a clarion, and anon sinking to the lowest, gentlest tones, thrilled the soul and sounded depths within men which perhaps in their case may never be touched by mortal speech?

When time permitted, De Koven played a wider role in the affairs of the Episcopal Church. In 1868 he first became a deputy to the General Convention. This was a period, not unlike our own, of intense partisanship, and De Koven quickly found himself at the center of several disputes. He was an ardent advocate of Christian education and worked against efforts to curtail ritualism.

At the General Convention of 1871 De Koven was the acknowledged leader of the ritualists. Two brilliant and clever speeches defeated proposed canons that would have prohibited a number of ritual practices, some of which implied belief in the "Real Presence" of Christ in the Holy Eucharist, which De Koven defended. Three years later he again helped defeat a move toward ritual uniformity. Thereafter, the Episcopal Church practiced the broad tolerance of ceremonial that exists today. James De Koven was now the most widely discussed figure in the Church.

But he was forced to pay a bitter price for his defense of principle. Opponents blocked five attempts to make him a Bishop.

From 1866, when he was nominated to be Bishop Coadjutor of Wisconsin, through 1875, when Standing Committees failed to approve his election as Bishop of Illinois, De Koven's name was vilified and condemned by those who equated ritualism with "papal abominations." In a struggle over the bishopric of his home diocese, he was attacked by former colleagues at Nashotah House and three leading rectors of the diocese. The emotional toll on this gentle and pious man was considerable and may well have hastened his death. He told a student, "Mere success is a poor thing. Duty is everything. It is singular but true, you know, that of all the clergy in the Church, I am the only one who can never hope under any circumstances of becoming a bishop."

At the General Convention of 1877, only two deputies supported De Koven's call, on behalf of the diocese of Wisconsin, for a Constitutional Commission to strike the words "Protestant Episcopal" as the legal title of the Church.

At a diocesan council meeting the following year, he defended the Cathedral movement and Bishop Welles, who had championed the "See principle" in Wisconsin. The controversy was such that De Koven confided to his superior, "Bishop, I did not close my eyes last night. This strain and worry is more than I am able to bear. I must go home. I do not believe that I shall be able to come to a council again."

He declined calls from the prestigious Trinity parish in New York and the Church of the Advent in Boston. A sister urged him to accept the bid from Trinity, arguing that his health could be improved were he freed of the burdens placed upon him by the College, the diocese, and the General Convention. But De Koven replied, "Much as I should like to accept, I shall never leave Racine. My duty is *here.*"

On an early morning in the winter of 1879, De Koven suffered a broken ankle on an icy Milwaukee street and was unable to summon help for half an hour. He seemed to recover well, but four weeks later, on March 19, he died suddenly of a heart attack. He left Racine College all that he owned.

A blinding snowstorm could not prevent a huge crowd containing eight Bishops from attending the funeral service on March 22.

The Rev. Dr. Sullivan of Trinity Church, Chicago, said: "In no life that has anywhere come under my observation have I ever seen a more perfect illustration of that striking phrase of the Psalmist, 'The beauty of holiness,' for in it there was nothing to repel from the Christian life, but everything to win, to woo, and attract. His was not the purity of the snow that chills, but of the sunlight that gladdens, warms, and vivifies." The student newspaper editorialized, "Too much of praise cannot be bestowed upon him. Each attempt of the most intellectual men of our day, falls far short of presenting him to us as we have known and loved him."

Racine College declined steadily after De Koven's death and was brought to a halt as a junior college in 1933 by the Great Depression. Its dilapidated buildings were purchased in 1935 by the De Koven Foundation for Church Work, created by the Community of St. Mary. The Sisters restored much of the 40-acre campus and today operate it as a facility for retreats and conferences. De Koven's tomb, next to his beloved St. John's Chapel, remains a source of inspiration to visitors from all over the world.

It is hoped that the following selections, taken from De Koven's *Sermons Preached On Various Occasions* (published in 1880 and long out-of-print) will remind us of the life and faith of a man who enriched the lives of many and reopened the Episcopal Church to the beauty and piety of its Catholic heritage.

T. C. R.

I

FIRST OF ALL, my brother, from the depth of your misery, from your knowledge that it is misery, and yet from that knowledge, most oppressive of all, that you do not feel it to be misery; from the very consciousness that you are not fit to pray, that you know not how to pray, that you cannot pray—still, pray. Pray to Him to pray for you; pray to Him to give you a broken and contrite heart; pray to Him to lift up your eyes unto that Hill of Calvary whence alone cometh your help; and He will hear and answer you.

There is a sight of Christ crucified given to the faithful, which alone is healing, alone is life-giving. It is in that very Sacramental Bread from which the sinner turns with loathing. There is Christ present, not visible to the eye, not to be appreciated by the senses, not in any carnal or material fashion, but truly, really there—Priest and sacrifice, ready to forgive, ready to pardon, ready to help. To come to the Holy Communion, beloved, in faith and penitence, is to come to Christ. It is to kneel at His feet, to have His hand laid upon you, to be sprinkled with His blood, to be fed with Himself. Oh! did we believe this, could we turn away from it so readily, could we come to it so carelessly, could we desire it so seldom, could we esteem it so lightly?

Work for God more enduring, more availing, has been done by loving, personal, individual dealing with particular souls, than by all eloquent sermons and soul-stirring oratory.

Men sometimes think they have no influence; but there is no one so poor, or weak, or untrained, or unworthy, but there is some one else who derives either good or evil from his existence. And here is the terrible thought: a man's influence does not come from what he seems to be, not from what he thinks he is, not from what he would like to have others think of him, not from his public reputation—from nothing but his real character . . . to your mother and to your father, to the wife of your bosom, to your son and daughter, to him or her whom you love the best on earth, you are, so far as your influence goes, not what you seem to be, but what you really are—a life-giving power, or a moral pestilence.

The truest obedience is only learned by suffering. Our Blessed Lord Himself learned obedience by the things which He suffered, and so it is evermore with His children. Tribulation and patience are the parents of obedience, and obedience is at once the mother and the child of love. The bruised soul pours forth the sweetness of charity, just as they say, in the far-off East, from the broken leaves of the spice-plant flows out the sweetest fragrance.

Here, we grow by fits and starts, by ebbs and flows; here, we grow by stumblings and falls and retrogressions; here, we grow by pain and anguish, and distress and misery. There, the sunshine of God's countenance ever falls brighter and brighter; there, the Lamb which is in the midst of the throne feeds them and leads them unto living fountains, and wipes away all tears from their eyes.

. . . the life of the baptized Christian is a life of struggle, and was meant so to be. He was to crucify the flesh with its affections and lusts; the life of the Christian was to be a life of warfare, if he would win the crown. But it was to be a life of conquest as well. By prayer, by the Bible, by Confirmation, by the offered Eucharist, by the feeding of the soul with Christ's Body and Blood, by the perpetual worship of Christ's invisible presence, the Christian was to be more than conqueror. Nay, by humiliation, and repentance, and confession, and absolution, his very sins and falls were to be made the stepping-stones to higher virtues.

Have you ever thought why, in many cases, God sends sorrow and affliction and misery upon His servants? One has pain of body, uneasy days, restless nights; another has anguish of mind, and spiritual darkness and desolateness of soul; another has children, and dear ones, and friends taken away; another lives in poverty and humiliation, and in the scorn and contumely of men. Do you know why these things come? It is because Christ loves His children, and seeks to give them, even by pain and anguish, the knowledge of Him and the knowledge of themselves. Happy they who hear his voice, and see Him and their own condition, even when He thus speaks to them.

How solitary, after all, is the real life of each human being. We are born alone, we must die alone. In our deepest trials, as far as human help goes, we must stand by ourselves. I do not say this as undervaluing sympathy and love and kindness, which go so far to alleviate sorrow, but merely as expressing the thought that sympathy and love and kindness have their limits. Even in that highest and best of all human relationships, to which God has given a sacramental glory, and which He has made the type of the union of Christ and His Church—the consecrated union of man and wife— even where there is the fullest sympathy and love, there is a point in which each stands apart from the other. The life of each individual being is in some sort a hidden life. There are heights and depths in human nature which are hidden and covered from every eye but the All-seeing gaze. Man is made in the image of God, though that image is marred. The baptized man has been recreated in that image; he has been made a member of Christ, a child of God, and an heir of the kingdom of heaven. There are capacities in his regenerate nature which can never be fully brought out, until that regeneration is completed by the redemption of the body. Meanwhile the struggle is going on between regenerated man and the world, the flesh and the devil. With whatever helps counsel or advice or prayer may give, he fights his battle alone. He puts on his armor. With sword and shield and helmet he enters the lists. Myriads, indeed, are watching him; hosts upon hosts behold him. The Eternal Eye is upon him; the loving Master sees him, and strengthens and supports; and human prayers, with agonizing entreaty, intercede for him; but still, so far as his fellow man is concerned, he fights alone. Nor does he merely fight and conquer. He fights and falls, he rises and falls again, and falls and rises. He is covered with wounds, and blood, and soil, and stain, until the day is done, and the crown is won or lost.

My brethren, let us learn . . . the great benefit of plainness, and simplicity, and honest truthfulness; the benefit of seeking to appear just what we are—no better, no worse. Let us learn, too, to bear injustice, and misconception, and want of appreciation with quiet calmness; because so soon it will all be right. Let us learn also the great benefit of the honest shame, that takes away shame, in the penitent acknowledgement of sin; judging ourselves, that we be not judged of the Lord. And last of all, let us seek, even while we have earthly blessings, and are thankful for them, in the midst of summer days and happy hours—much more, in times of trouble and distress—to have our hearts safely stored with Him who knows all that we are, and accepts, not because of what we are, but because with humble penitence we put our trust in Him.

. . . true Christian hope, once let it dwell in the soul, no storm or tempest, no billows or waves can ever move you. The loss of friends, hardest of earthly trials, can never overwhelm you, for you sorrow not as others which have no hope. Death itself, with the darkness of its shadow, the coldness of its waves, the long, weary time of waiting which it brings, can never separate you from the love of Christ; for even your very flesh, as the Psalmist tells you, "shall rest in hope." Bury the body deep down in the earth, scatter its ashes to the four winds of heaven, sink it beneath the caverns of the sea, still Hope shall tenderly care for it and quicken it with invisible life, and waken it at the resurrection morning.

How many parents . . . have in their households those blessed influences of family religion which used to be so common—I mean family prayers, morning and evening; the going to church twice on Sunday, as a family; such measure of attendance at weekday services as is possible; the Sunday catechizing of the children, not delegated to irresponsible Sunday-school teachers, but done by father and mother in person? . . . Among the many boys who have been under my charge, I have been led to remark the marvelous difference which exists between those who have had such religious help as this at home, and those who have not. Such loving care, at least, protects from grosser sin. It becomes to the unprotected youth like the sheltering wings of invisible angels, and holy words and blessed prayers, and even half-unheeded teachings, go before and around him, like an armed host. I believe that parents rarely realize how great are the temptations to which even very little children are exposed. I do not believe they realize how powerless they themselves are, even with the best of care, to keep their children out of temptation; but, if they can send with them, wherever they go, the awful protection of heavenward-ascending prayers, and the majestic power of holy text and harmonious hymn, the powers of evil are frighted away.

There is nothing in this fair earth, nothing amid all the costly jewels of the Bride of Christ, so glorious, so beautiful, ay, so awe-inspiring, as a true Christian boy. Early baptized, duly trained, sheltered by prayer, molded by obedience, pure and manly, of open brow and fearless glance, strengthened by Confirmation, for ever quickened and renewed by the Body and Blood of the Lord who died for him, he is a blessing and a comfort, a strength and support, a lesson and an example, to us all.

Education, to be real education, must include the training of body, mind, and soul coordinately, and neglect no one of them. The intellectual training, therefore, which leaves God out of it, which imagines that any study, however abstract, can be pursued without Him as its beginning and end, must end in intellectual death. It may take long to die, but it can have only one result.

. . . There are three factors in the educational problem: the immortal being who is instructed, the immortal being who instructs, and, far inferior to both of them, the book or books which are used in instruction. Banish religion from the latter, if you will; drive away the immortal works upon whose pages are written "For the honor and glory of God," if you can; but so long as the instructor is a believing man, and the soul of the pupil is ready to receive his instructions, just so long it must be religious education. I care not what the subject is, though it be the most abstract problem of the purest science, the living soul of the teacher, informed by the Eternal Word, pours into the living soul of the pupil that light "of God in which alone we see light." Banish God and the truth of God from such instruction! As well might you try to banish the sunlight from the upseeking glance of tree and shrub and flower. Men who really teach cannot help themselves. It is not the word only that teaches; it is the glance and movement and all the soul of him that instructs; and, if he be a Christian, it is Christian teaching. Hence, so long as the land is a believing land, and its people are a people of believers, and its teachers hold to the truths of Christianity, is its instruction religious instruction.

Not simply through faith in Christ, not simply through love of Christ, not simply through zeal for Christ, not simply by the conforming of heart and will to His, do Christians grow nearer to one another; but through oneness with Him on earth, in the Church His Body, through the Sacraments in the same holy Church; in Paradise, by His own blessed and life-giving presence. As Christians thus grow nearer to Him, they ever grow nearer to one another.

Do you know what it is to worship . . . the Incarnate Son of God, who not only sits at the right hand of the Father, but in the Church and in His sacraments, reveals His hidden glory? Ye worship God, ye think; but do ye worship God in Christ? The awful touch of God made man, the body of Christ, which is the Church of God—its powers and mysteries and sacraments, its guidance and strength and comfort, because everywhere in it is the hidden presence of Jesus—this is our refuge from that backward course which leads by slow but sure steps from Christianity to Judaism, from Judaism to the denial of a personal God, until the horror-stricken soul, burning, longing, desiring, stands face to face with the blank darkness of materialism.

I know, indeed, that the devil has his ministers as well as Christ. There are those who seem filled with an eager desire to make others as evil as themselves. Nay, it is sometimes appalling to witness how much more in earnest is the messenger of Satan than the Christian bought with the blood of Jesus. With what hesitation and feebleness, and fear of offending, will the latter seek to win a soul to Christ, while the former knows neither fear nor hesitation nor lack of opportunity.

Seek, then, for the two gifts which chiefly made him what he was—Christian courage and Christian love. We live in an age when cowardice in religious matters has been dignified into a virtue. Pray to God to make you bold to do his will. Dare to give up the world, with its pomps and its pleasure and vain applause. Be not afraid of its sneers or laughter, or, what one needs to dread much more, its tenderness and anxiety and solicitude. It will applaud you as long as you echo its own tone, but it cries out against fasting and prayer, and obedience and penitence, and the ever-recurring Eucharist. Dare to believe in Christ and the Bride of Christ, and to practice what you believe.

The world demands success; God only asks for labor. The world clamors for results; God asks for principles. Whether His servants succeed or fail in the eyes of men, is a thing altogether immaterial in His sight, if only they do their part well, and hand on the witness of the truth from age to age. They are to be the champions of the right, happen what may.

I hope I shall not be thought satirical, if I say that the members of our Church are prevented from giving the large gifts which one hears of elsewhere by the fact that it costs more to support the average Episcopalian, and to keep him and his in that "station of life unto which it has pleased God to call him," than it has done any other kind of Christian since the time when the Divine Master declared "that the foxes have holes, and the birds of the air have nests, but the Son of Man hath not where to lay His head." Perhaps I may add that, owing it may be to the generally comfortable tone which prevails, the sort of well-to-do, refined, cultivated, worldly Christianity, nothing which does not reflect the average tone of thought, feeling, doctrine, and idea that is prevalent, can expect to be aided by what liberality there is. Anything beyond this can only look for an amiable toleration, with the permission to succeed if it be able to do so, and may be most thankful if it can avoid actual misrepresentation, and that species of persecution which is popular in an age tolerant of everything excepting the Faith.

Sturdy doubting admits of being vanquished. Sometimes even the amount of the doubt is the measure of the faith of which the same soul is capable. More dangerous is the spirit that thinks all religious views worthy of equal consideration, because all are alike unworthy of any; which is tolerant, because it cares for nothing; which substitutes for disbelief the worse error that belief or unbelief, religion or irreligion, faith or doubt, are alike unimportant considerations; which dreams that all pursuits, all studies, all training can be accomplished as well without religion as with it; and which, by ignoring the spiritual world, fancies that it has been gotten rid of. But, mighty and vast, the spiritual world stretches around us, with its heights and depths, with its shadows and dreams, with its angels and spirits, with its heavens and hell, with its eternal voices and its unending felicities. It is governed by its own laws and its own principles, and these, too, in strict harmony with the laws of nature and of mind. The soul, spiritual and immortal, needs, and its very being craves, these laws and principles. Vainly we dredge the ocean, or climb the Andes, or are parched beneath the torrid sun, or penetrate the frozen seas, if mightier heights and depths, and frozen hearts, and fevered souls, move us not to labors as earnest.

But Adam fell, and we inherit a fallen nature. It needs no proof. What parent that has had the care of children; what teacher that has tried to train the young; nay, what human being who once has inspected his own heart and known the depths of moral evil of which it is capable, will venture to deny this? Not totally fallen, not entirely depraved. God forbid! The conscience which still remains in unregenerate man, the freedom of the will, the burning longing after God and the unseen, which never have ceased to

assert themselves, are proofs of this. Nor will it satisfy either the
thoughtful reasoner or earnest lover of his kind, to be told that
the religion of Socrates, the temperance of Zeno, the justice of
Aristides, the patriotism of Regulus, the continence of Scipio, the
vast powers of a Caesar, were only a development of the fidelity of
the dog, the local attachment of the cat, the affection of the mon-
key, and vast victories of some conquering hordes of rats; any
more than it will to require us to believe, against all our sense of
what is true and just, that these were but works of the devil,
totally corrupt. Nay, fallen nature stands like some fair ruin—arch,
and pillar, and buttress, mighty stones which none can move,
beautiful carving which none can surpass; but, as you gaze more
nearly, and tear away the ivy that makes decay so beautiful, lo!
lizards crawl upon the walls, and the wind blows rudely through
the mullioned windows, and the stones crumble slowly away; and
in all its glory, and in all its beauty, it is a ruin.

The hidden curse of most men is selfishness, with all its morbid
brood of self-consciousness, conceit, vanity, littleness, and feebleness. It is the explanation of too many failures in men of whom
one expects better things.

. . . be loyal to something, not yourself; to an abstraction, an
idea, a notion, if you can do no better; to your father and mother,
to your friend or your teacher, to the woman you love, to a priest
or a statesman, to the man who embodies some great cause, and
suffers for it! Forget yourself and your own interest, your faults,
your sins, your virtues, your wants, your hopes, your fears, and
find in this forgetfulness of self a deeper knowledge, a purer aim,
a more enduring reward.

. . . Is the tendency of the age upward or downward? Are we
growing better or worse? Are we, on the whole, purer, more unselfish, more free from evil motives, possessed of that element of
strength which high morality always gives, because it is based on
self-denial, self-command, and continence? I will not ask merely
whether one hears of more evil than of old, for that may be only a

result of what is miscalled the liberty of the press—a liberty whereby our sons and daughters can read of every foul deed with which this earth is polluted; but I will ask, whether there are not sins and offenses, not only practiced, but beginning to find eager and subtle defenders, which strike a blow at honor, at manliness, at all that is best and noblest, at family life, at virtue, at strength, at national power? Can you not trace corruption in art, in poetry, in the home, in government, in religion?

. . . what better words of counsel can I give you than to bid you to hold fast to that Saviour into whom you were grafted in Baptism, who has fed you with Himself in the Blessed Eucharist? Live for Christ; live in Christ; seek Him by penitence; find Him in His Eucharist. Die in Him; die for Him! Count no labor worth the effort which has not His mark upon it; fight His battles, gain His victories. Then in the shadow of death He will support you, and in the day of Judgment succor you, and make you reign with Him in that new-born earth for which the weary world is waiting.

To surrender the will, to humble the pride, to become like a little child; to believe in the unseen; to know that there is another world than that about us, to enter it by Baptism, to live in it by the Holy Communion; to be guided by the voice and hand of an invisible Master; to be drawn nearer and nearer to that blessed Home of which death is only the portal; to see the solemn pageant of the world's great activities go marching by as in a spectacle; to be in it, yet far above it; to despise none of its beauty or goodness or excellence, and yet to have the life hid with Christ in God; above its din and noise, to hear celestial harmonies; in the midst of his hurry and bustle, to be at peace; to care neither for its honors nor its persecutions; sober in prosperity, patient and resigned in adversity, at rest in life, at rest in death, one with Christ for ever— this is the victory that overcometh the world, even our faith!

SPIRITUAL BLINDNESS

(Preached at Racine, 1859)

"And when they saw Him, they began to pray Him to
depart out of their coasts." — St. Mark v. 17.

THE TEXT, BELOVED, presents to our view a story of sorrow and of
sin. Our Blessed Lord had crossed the Sea of Galilee into the
country of the Gadarenes. He had been asleep in the hinder part
of the ship while the waves were beating high. The disciples had
cried, "Save, Lord, or we perish," and He had rebuked the winds
and bade the angry waves be still. But a wilder storm than the
wrath of the elements awaited Him. An unhappy demoniac, in
whose soul was the bitter contest between the powers of evil and
the spirit of a man, came forth to meet Him. Sad indeed is the
history which St. Mark gives of his condition. No longer amid the
walks of men, amid the joys of home or the sounds of the busy
world, had he his dwelling. It will be remembered that it was the
custom of the Jews to bury their dead outside the walls of the
city, in caves or sepulchres hewn out of the rock. It was in these
tombs, as we read, that he had his abode. Amid the silence of the
dead, amid bones and skeletons and pallid faces, amid winding-
sheets and the damp of death, he dwelt. Ofttimes they had bound
him with fetters and chains, but such was his mighty strength that
they were but as feeble bands. The traveler feared to pass that way,
and no sound broke the solemn stillness but his pacing up and
down, the living among the dead, and his cries of horror, louder
than the beating of the waves upon the lonely shore, as he cut
himself with stones until the blood gushed out afresh.

He it was who, perhaps with hostile thought, perhaps allured to
Him who was to draw all men unto Him, came down to meet our
Lord as He landed on the coasts of Gadara. Whatever his motive, he
is met by the command of the Ruler of all, "Come out of him,
thou unclean spirit." Evermore, in the soul of the demoniac, is a
fearful contest. On the one hand he falls and worships the Master;
on the other he cries aloud, "What have I to do with Thee, Jesus

thou Son of God?" Evil and good strive within him. He comes
unto the Lord, and yet the foul spirit adjures Him to torment him
not. He would fain dwell longer in the earthly tabernacle, and
make a sport of the human soul. But the stronger than the strong
has come upon him, to bind and to loose. The captive is free, the
prisoner is unbound, the chain is broken by Him, mighty to save.

One thing the legion of unclean spirits can obtain. Bereft of their
human habitation, they would fain dwell in the herd of swine that
feed by the banks of the lake. If not the nature of man, at least
the bestial nature, they would seek to influence. But mark how
evil ever outwits itself. The whole herd, actuated by the strange
impulse, ran violently down a steep place and perished in the
waters. And they that kept them fled, and told in the city and in
the country what had befallen to him who was possessed with the
devil, and to the swine.

We naturally ask, What was the result? Did they not come forth
with songs of joy and branches of palm-trees to meet the Deliverer
who had freed their countryman from a calamity so awful? Had
they any other thought than to bid Him welcome who thus visibly
proclaimed Himself their God? Did not their hearts beat with a
deeper joy when they heard of the mighty conquest? Alas! no.
They had lost their worldly goods. The herd that fed upon the
shores of the lake was a goodly possession. It was worth so much,
and it was a loss, a total loss. A strange fear possessed them. What
if this were but a beginning? What if the presence of this mighty
stranger should bring other losses with it. What if poverty and
hunger were to accompany his spiritual blessings? What, after all,
were grace and holiness, and demons cast out, and penitents
absolved, to the loss of worldly goods? Money could buy, money
made them respectable, money could clothe and feed them; and
what could these other things do? Christ and holiness were too
expensive for the people of Gadara. Thus they reasoned, and thus
they acted; for "when they saw Him they besought Him to depart
out of their coasts." With hands uplifted to bless, they will not
take the benediction. With words of comfort on His lips, they will
not hear Him. With the Gospel of salvation offered them, they
beseech Him to depart. And He took them at their word; He heard

their desire, He granted their request; He left them, and departed. Alas for the city of Gadara! Alas for the land beyond the sea! A deeper loss than ever before has befallen them! The fields may be as glad and gay as ever; men may laugh and be merry as they did aforetime; the world may be just as busy, and men richer than before; but Christ is gone, Jesus is no longer there. The waves shall beat upon the shore for ages, and storm and calm, full many a time, pass over the waters of the Sea of Galilee; but never shall He who rules the winds and waves, and the raging hearts of men, bless them again with His bodily presence.

It is a fearful instance, indeed, of a desire granted, of a prayer heard, to the loss of those who made it; of a spiritual blindness that met with a spiritual punishment, awful indeed. You must notice that the sin of the Gadarenes was not unbelief. They had not the excuse that they did not acknowledge the Lord as a mighty being. It was rather that, knowing Him to be such, seeing His mighty works, for fear of the worldly loss He brought with Him, they besought Him to depart. In other words, the state of the Gadarenes and their sin is just the state and the sin of the majority of those who come to church nowadays, and hear the Word of God; and, perhaps, what is a thing indeed to be pondered, it may be punished in the same way.

Do you ever think, beloved, that while you may not reject Christ you may beseech Him to depart from you, and He may hear and answer your prayer?

The majority of people have a belief in Christ. They have a certain amount of good about them. They mean to be holy by and by. They have the idea of Baptism or Confirmation and a devout life as a thing for the future. But there is something that keeps them back—some loss that they feel they must endure; something that they must give up—some pleasure, some sin; some honor, some employment; some restitution to make, a cross to bear, a self-denial to endure, a life in the world but not of it—and they can not do it.

There is one thing, however, in the life of all, which comes especially as an instance of the history of the text. The spiritual life of a man is a strange thing. That life which is between each man's soul and God has a mysterious history. If it be true that man is made in the image of God, though that image be marred, if it be true that "the light of God lighteneth every man that cometh into the world," if it be true that God wills that all men should be saved, we must know that God speaks to the soul of every man; that He has a message for each man's need, a Gospel of glad tidings for every creature under heaven, that there is no one whom God at some time or other has not mercifully tried to bring unto Himself. In some way suited to the capacity of each, God has spoken and called by His Spirit. I suppose there is no one before me who is not conscious of this—that he might have been a Christian man if he would; that Christ has stood near him, and stretched out His hand unto him, and called him gently, although he did not answer; that Christ has stood, as it were, in his very coasts—in the church, in his home, in his place of business. And the reason why He is no longer with him is because he besought Him to depart.

Perhaps there is no period of life when the advent of Christ to the soul of man, if I may call it so, seems to come so evidently as to the child, just entering into manhood. Whether he be baptized or unbaptized, whether it be the speaking of the grace already within him or the voice of God's ineffable election, Christ stands by his side. His voice is very gentle, His accents most loving. He lays his hand upon his brow and almost leads him with His love. His words are like the sound of many waters, and harpers harping with their harps. It would only be a little self-government, the restraint of the passions, the life by rule, the steady habit of duty, reverence, obedience, and devotion; and he almost tries it. But life is sunny, and hopes are bright, and the world seems strewed with flowers; and, half sorrowful, he falls at the feet of his Lord, and beseeches Him to depart. And he leaves him, for a little while, to himself and the busy world.

He grows older and stronger, and is more full of manhood and power. The world, indeed, is not so bright as it was, but it more fills his soul. He works, and is strong; he eats, and is satisfied. Busy action delights him. He is tempted, and he sins; there are spots on his soul: the prayers of his childhood, the simplicity of his boyhood—they are gone. But all the while Christ beholds him; He loves him still; He watches him every day, and once more He stands by his side. It is in the height of his happiness, it may be, in the tenderness of his love, in the first joy of a father's heart, in the brightness of his promise, that He calls him. But can he leave the world and its pleasures? Can he leave the pursuit of gain? Can he become humble as a little child? Nay, it is too deep a loss, and once more he bids Him depart.

He is middle-aged now, and his locks are somewhat silvered. His passions are tamed and his blood runs coldly. Nothing excites him greatly, but he lives in the routine of his business. He is a man of habits. He does every day what he did yesterday. His dreams are over, and realities beset him. Things have disappointed him, and he thinks much of his comfort. There is a charm about his home and his children. It is a quiet place for him, where he can rest. There at least he is sure of sincerity and truth and unselfish love, and there his heart centers. It is there, once more, with chastising love, the Master meets him. He can only be made perfect through suffering. The grave yawns for his loved ones. It is the fair child or the wife beloved that he must bury out of his sight. By the side of the open grave, in the midst of his sorrow and his heart-broken anguish, once more he sees that form divine. He hears the only words that can comfort him. A vision of that love, better than of sons and daughters, flashes upon him. But it is but for a moment: earth is too strong for him, and he beseeches Him to depart.

Age, weary age, is upon him. His staff will hardly support him as he totters along. Sadly, sadly pass the days, cold and desolate. There is a voice in his ear saying evermore, "Earth to earth, dust to dust!" Father and mother and early friends, where are they? Hopes and expectations, and the aims of youth, what have they come to? Life, life, what has it been? In the wakeful nights memory torments him. Ghosts of sins long since committed haunt him. Melancholy shapes beset him. As one that stands upon the seashore, with impassable rocks behind, and sees the advancing tide that shall overwhelm, and hears no sound of answer but the ceaseless beating of the waves and the wild cry of the sea-birds, so he stands on the brink of eternity. The years of his life stretch out before him; they mock him with their emptiness. Like a spectral host they march along, and as they pass by, one by one, cry aloud with accents of terror, "Lost, for ever!"

He knows it not, perchance, but, veiled in wrath, still Christ is standing by him. His very remorse is the voice of the Lord. It is the last opportunity, the last hour of his probation, the last effort of mercy. Will he let Him go away, with heaven and hell before him, and the grave open at his feet? Alas! He is passing by. There is no sound that bids Him stay; no voice that says, "Abide with me"; no hand that touches the hem of His garment; no supplicating cry, "Jesus, Master, have mercy on me!" Will no one warn him? can friend nor brother help him? shall the Lord pass out of his coasts for ever? Close his eyes gently, and part his silver hair upon his forehead, and cross his hands upon his bosom, and say your prayers, and write his epitaph, for all is over—over until you and I and the people of Gadara, with kindreds and nations and languages, shall see Him once again in the clouds of heaven.

Oh! my brethren, I beseech you to ponder the matter most carefully. God is very merciful, but we may slight His mercies. He may be calling you now, and you may be asking Him to depart. Is there no voice speaking at your hearts that you gain would silence? It will take but a little effort, and He will go away from you. Pleasure, and gayety, and business, and making money—there are ten thousand ways of bidding Him depart. But do you desire to lose Him? Are you sure He will ever come again? Would you wish Him to take you at your word? Is the little you will make by it worth such a loss? Is the world, after all, the better portion? Were the people of Gadara better off than the persecuted disciples?

Oh! if Christ is calling you now, in this Lenten season, by the voice of nature or the voice of grace, by joy or sorrow, at home or in the church, in whatever way it may be, now, in this approaching Confirmation, kneel at His feet and say, "Lord, help me." And the answer will be yours: "Go in peace; thy sins are forgiven thee." For He is ever repeating the promise: "Behold, I stand at the door and knock; if any man will open unto me, I will come in unto him, and sup with him, and he with Me."

The Gates of the Invisible

(Preached at Racine College, Ash Wednesday, 1878)

"He endured, as seeing Him who is invisible."
Heb. xi., part of verse 27.

ST. PAUL IS SPEAKING of the faith of Moses. He refused to be called the son of Pharaoh's daughter. He chose rather to suffer affliction with the people of God than to enjoy the pleasures of sin for a season. He forsook Egypt, not fearing the wrath of the king. He esteemed the reproach of Christ greater riches than the treasures in Egypt. He gave up all that could make life happy or beautiful; he bore a burden heavy to be borne of weary ruling of a disobedient people. But of whatever he gave up, or whatever he did, this was the secret motive: "He endured, as seeing Him who is invisible."

Not Moses alone. The long line of those of whom the world was not worthy, whether in high or low degree, subduing kingdoms, waxing valiant in fight, or made strong out of weakness—in cities and on thrones, in the wilderness and the desert, in quiet home or crowded mart, whatever their labor or suffering for God—had no other stay or strength than this, that they saw Him who is invisible.

To-day, when the Church is arrayed in sackcloth, when she bids us fast and weep if we will hear her voice, when she calls us to the poor measures of self-denial which we substitute for the toils of saints, if we mean anything by it—if we have any idea that it is of any use, if any chord in our hearts answers back to the solemn gloom of Ash-Wednesday, it is worthwhile to consider the only motive which can make self-denial tolerable, or anything, indeed, but a vain asceticism—seeing Him who is invisible.

We are surrounded by the visible; it hems us in on every side; the necessary duties of life are occupied with that which we see. Raiment to put on, food to eat, a house to live in, the care of our bodies, the sleep of night, the things which make up the warp and woof of our lives, belong to the visible. Our very intellectual work, so far as it has a practical result, belongs to what we see. To make men more capable of holding their own, of making money, of taking a high place in the world, of building railways, of conducting vast enterprises, nay, of leading armies and guiding states, is only, after all, to make them capable of doing their part well in this visible world. Nay, the things that seem most divine, the skill of painters, the harmony of musicians, the immortal works of historians, philosophers, and poets, are only transitory after all. If they last as long as the world lasts, it will not be for ever. I do not mean but that all these things, the humblest as well as the greatest, may not be made a means of access to the invisible; but this, after all, depends not on the work itself, but on the motive with which it is done. That which elevates it out of the region of the visible is something in itself invisible. It is some great hidden power, like faith, or love, or prayer, or fortitude, or insight, or the blending of them all. In this light, a common household duty done from the love of God, in the history which the angels write of men and life, may have in it a more lasting glory than the dome of St. Peter's, or the Sistine Madonna, or the masses of Mozart, or the plays of Shakespeare.

It is true, too, that there was never an age of the world when the visible seemed to possess such claims upon our thoughts as now. There are two things which chiefly occupy men's minds: the one is material development, the other is the study of nature. To discover new countries; to build vast railways; to make the most of this earth of ours, by mining, by agriculture, by easy methods of transit; to send cultivation and civilization everywhere—these, though noble works and the most engrossing thought of the times, nevertheless belong to the visible. When they are accompanied with a coarse love of wealth, with the heaping up of money for money's sake or the sake of the power that it brings, they degrade almost as much, though in another way, as idleness, or sensuality, or the easy living of those of whom the Latin poet sings: "We are mere ciphers, born to consume the fruits of the earth, mere suitors of Penelope, base and effeminate subjects of Alcinous, to whom it was fair to sleep to the middle of the day, and to lull their cares to rest to the music of the lyre." For work, and toil, and weary days, and wrinkled brows, and vast results, are only one degree better than idleness, if there be not in the labor some higher principle than coarse materialism.

But what shall we say of the study of nature, the passionate love of science, the intense devotion which dredges the sea, and climbs the Andes, and traverses the deserts, and freezes in the arctic zone, or is parched at the hidden sources of the Nile or the Niger? To what end is it? If it be in the spirit of the often-quoted passage of St. Augustine, it is well. Augustine writes: "I asked the earth, and it said, 'I am not He'; and all that is upon it made the same confession. I asked the sea and the depths, and the creeping things that have life, and they answered, 'We are not thy God; look thou above us.' I asked the breezes and the gales; and the whole air with its inhabitants said to me, 'Anaximenes is in error; I am not God.' I asked the heaven, the sun, the moon, the starts. 'We, too,' said they, 'are not the God whom thou seekest.' And I said to all the creatures that surround the door of my fleshly senses, 'Ye have said to me of my God, that ye are not He; tell me somewhat of Him.' And with a great voice they exclaimed, 'He made us.' "

But it is not always in this spirit that nature is studied. The miracles of one age become the science of another. Law after law is discovered; what we once thought the direct working of the Father of all proves to be a mighty force, a law whose going out and coming in is changeless as the courses of the seasons or the rising and setting of the sun. Not only are discoveries made, but there seems to stretch before the laborious philosopher a boundless range of discoveries, the end of which we do not see. The voice that seemed to say, "Thus far shalt thou come, and no farther," recedes and recedes. Between us and God appear to come laws, and forces and powers, the duration and extent of which we can grasp and measure. The visible encroaches on the invisible. What, then, if these laws begin to take to us the place of God? What if we conceive of a primal force behind them all, a law anterior to all other laws, a dull, extended, brute, inanimate power, and substitute this for the personal, living, loving Father of us all—for Him of whom the Psalmist said, "My soul is athirst for God, yea, even for the living God: when shall I come to appear before the presence of God?"

Who can deny that these two are the tendencies of the day—the idolatry of wealth, and power, and mere knowledge, and material resources; and, in the more thoughtful and philosophic, the substitution for the personal Ruler of the universe of a force which, though invisible to the eye, can be grasped by the understanding, comprehended by the intellect, explained by scientific formula, and is incapable of causing or demanding love, or faith, or gratitude, or prayer?

Seeing Him who is invisible. How do we know there is anything beyond what we see? We touch, and feel, and hear, and comprehend; by what arguments can we prove that there is anything more than this? No spirit has passed before us and made the trembling flesh to creep; no angelic visitant has sung "Peace on earth, good will to man"; no transfigured form, with vesture glistening white, has filled us with a vision passing words; no voice has sounded in the ear, saying, "This is my beloved Son, hear Him." Gaze up into heaven as we will, the hosts upon hosts of angelic powers, thrones and dominions, cherubim and seraphim, and above them all the Eternal Triune God, do not reveal themselves to mortal gaze; and sun and moon and stars and heavy leaden clouds alone are manifest. Nay, if there be metaphysical arguments, or any other arguments, on which we depend for the proof of the being and existence of God, it is, after all, a mere matter of reason; and he who is gifted with a greater grasp of intellect has a fairer chance of being religious than the ignorant and uneducated. Nay, if the reason is to decide upon proof, and accept simply because it is satisfied, who shall blame him who rejects what another accepts, and is not satisfied with what convinces and persuades a differently constituted intellect? Of course, I do not wish to undervalue the use of reason, or the value of evidences, or the mighty power of the proofs of Christianity. I only wish to put them in their true position; they rather serve to confirm the faith than to proclaim it.

The invisible must not simply be proven, it must be seen. Consider for a moment. Whatever else is uncertain, we are conscious of our own personal existence; each man knows that he has a something which is his, and no other man's; which distinguishes him at once from the brute creation, and from all other human beings. It is that which he means when he uses the word "I." Years may pass, circumstances may alter, the outward appearance may so change that no one can recognize his identity; childhood may give way to youth, and youth to age; but wherever he is, whatever he is, he remains the same identical person. And this personality resides in what we call the soul. The knife of the anatomist can not discover it; it can not be found in the folds of the brain; it can not be detected in the throbbing pulsations of the heart. It is utterly invisible; it cannot be seen or felt or heard. And yet it needs no proof; it has not to be argued about; it admits of no denial. It is, and we know it is.

Moreover, we know that this invisible personality is immortal. We watch some loved one, dearer perhaps than life, drawing nearer and nearer unto death. We hope, and then despair, and hope again. At last they tell us that the end is drawing on; we do not dare to be away; we linger by the bedside, and watch, and pray, and listen to every sound, and count each long-drawn breath. It comes and goes; it grows feebler and more difficult. There is a silence; we hear it again. There is a longer pause—and all is still. The cold, still form of what was once our hope and stay, parent or child, wife or husband, lies before us; but the soul we loved, the personality of the dear one, that which made him what he was—we know it is not there. The dust has returned to the dust as it was, but the spirit is gone to the God who gave it.

Nor do we know the immortality of the soul alone. Whether we have the power to analyze its emotions, or are only conscious of them by the longing pain they cause, through hope and fear, love and hate, through every one of its varied desires, the invisible and immortal soul pleads, and longs for, and demands, and knows that it possesses and is possessed by an invisible, eternal, almighty, personal God. Beyond the tangible and the earthly, beyond the real and the material, the personal existing soul, because it is the creation of God and is made in His image, though that image be marred, reaches out to Him who made it. It sees the invisible. And yet this must be noted: it not only sees God, it sees itself. It finds itself polluted, foul, incapable of good, with longings after holiness, and no strength to do right. It has a vision of God's justice, and purity, and righteousness, and knows that it is fallen and lost, and the opposite of all this. Hence, while the belief in God has been as universal as the human race, and there live no people so besotted that they have not in some sort acknowledged Him, false religions and varied misbeliefs have expressed, at the same time, the longings of the soul, and the mists and the darkness which, because of the Fall, have come between it and God.

But this is not all. If it were, then we might be Deists, but could not be Christians. God has answered the longings of the soul. "God so loved the world, that He gave His only begotten Son, that whosoever believeth in Him should not perish, but have everlasting life." "The Word was made flesh, and dwelt among us (and we beheld His glory, the glory as of the only begotten of the Father), full of grace and truth." The Eternal God has revealed Himself to man in the person of Jesus Christ. Brethren, I preach Christ unto you today. He has been manifested to take away our sins. He was born, He lived, upon the Cross of Calvary He died for all; He conquered death, He rose again, He ascended into heaven, He lives for evermore. Nor in heaven alone—He lives on earth as well. He is in His Church; it is His Body. He speaks in His priests; He is with them all the day. He is in His Eucharists; they are His Body and Blood. The Lord Jesus Christ, whom the Magdalen touched, and St. John loved, and St. Peter denied, and Pilate crucified, and Roman soldiers spat upon, our Own, our God, is with us now.

Moreover, just as each human soul, because it is made in the image of God, longs for and beholds—though it be but to tremble— the Invisible God, so to every soul whom He calls to holy Baptism the Lord Jesus Christ, through the power of the Holy Ghost, gives Himself, and, with Himself, the gift of faith. We can believe, and we do believe, and see by faith the Eternal God, in the face of Jesus Christ—now, indeed, through a glass darkly—but behold Him still. As the Apostle says, "We all with unveiled face, beholding as in a mirror the glory of the Lord, are changed into the same image, from glory to glory, as by the spirit of the Lord."

Brethren, I say—I appeal to your own consciences to confirm it— that each baptized person before me has seen the Lord Jesus Christ— not with the bodily eye indeed, but with that which sees as clearly, the eye of faith. More than this, I say that he who before me is the least devout, the most unworthy, the most careless, has had this vision. Is there one in this congregation who does not know that at some time or another, once or twice or more—when, I cannot tell, but he knows—Christ has stood by him? Did He not call to you? Did He not speak to you? Did He not plead with you? Did He not show you His wounded hands? Did He not stand and wait when you bade Him go away? Was it when your mother or your father died? Was it when you were sick; Was it when you were bidden to Confirmation? Was it before the altar when the Mystical Presence flashed upon you? Was it in the stillness of the night, or at some time when nothing masked it except that He was there? Is it *now*, perhaps, my child—on this Ash Wednesday—as this Lent begins?

But perhaps you answer, "It is true, but I can not see Him now. Sin, and pleasure, and self-indulgence, and want of prayer, or some dark deed have driven Him away." I answer then, it was for this that the Church appointed the Lenten season. Faith, and prayer, and fasting and tears, and self-denial, and confession, and kneeling in His courts—these are the Gates of the Invisible. Once, with His help, open them, and within, patient and loving still, your Lord will stand.

The mists that hide that Form, beloved, from you are of your own making. Deeds of faith, and mortifying the flesh, will drive them away, and the Sun of Righteousness appear. Then, when once you really behold the Saviour, in the words of the text, you can and will endure. The temptations of the passions, the assaults of unbelief, the opinion of the world, the snares of the devil—nay, sorrow, calamity, afflictions, poverty, and death—can be borne and resisted, in a strength and power which is not your own. The light of that countenance will illumine all things, and make you strong in your very weakness. Over these daily temptations, these hourly falls, this prayerlessness and weakness and want of love, will come the victory. Nay, as days grow darker, and the gloom increases, when the feet stumble and the valley of the shadow surrounds, with the eye fixed on Him, and an ever clearer vision of His perfections, we shall see Him as He is, and, awaking up after His likeness, shall be satisfied with it.

Men of Understanding

(Preached at an Ordination in 1874)

"Men that had understanding of the times, to know
what Israel ought to do." — I Chron. xii., part of
verse 32.

IT IS ONE OF THE notes of the Church of God that it has a marvelous
adaptation to different times, circumstances, and races. Unvarying
as to the unchanging faith, she draws forth from her treasures
things new and old. The Tree of Life, ever from the one root,
through the one stock, from branch and twig, and stem, she is
throwing out, with unfailing vitality, leaf after leaf for the healing
of the nations. Because she is the body and spouse of Christ,
because in her indwells the Eternal Spirit, she has a certain fitness
for every possible situation in which she may be placed. She has a
remedy for every ill, a relief for every want, an answer to every cry.
Slavery and freedom, barbarism and civilization, peace and war,
learning and ignorance, are alike, to her, only providential means
of helping onward the children of men. She is like her Divine Lord,
now in the midst of the doctors, now in the carpenter's shop, now
in the crowded city, now on the lonely mountain-top, now casting
a pitying glance on Magdalen, now denouncing woe on scribe and
Pharisee, now bending in agony, now in the midst of innumerable
hosts of angels; yet ever, from the glance of her eye, from the
intercession of her prayers, from the sternness of her wrath, from
the majesty of her triumph, from the wail of her humiliation, nay,
even from the hem of her garment, and her very shadow as she
passes, sending forth strength, and healing, and peace.

Of this characteristic of the Church, her ministry must, in a
measure, be sharers. Whatever she is, she is only it because she is
the body of Christ. Because He lives, she lives also; in Him she lives
and moves and has her being, and they too, as members of Him
and of her—His body and spouse—partake of her powers and
energies. This indeed is true of all Christians, but of the ministry
it is more especially true, because to them is a promise of Christ's
presence and indwelling beyond that which is given to other men.

To them He says, "Lo, I am with you always, even unto the end of the world." In short, as there never has arisen, and never can arise, any possible event or conditions, from the fall to the hour of judgment, for which she is not the refuge and stay of man, so in every age and all circumstances must and will her ministry be "Men of understanding of the times, to know what Israel ought to do."

In taking up the subject which the Church, by the rubrics in the Ordinal, imposes upon me, I think I shall be complying with the spirit of its direction if I consider under what conditions the ministry must be exercised, if one would be a "man of understanding of the times." And yet I must guard myself, at once, against a possible misapprehension. The Christian clergyman a time-server? God forbid! To truckle to the spirit of the age, to submit to the tone of the day, to make no protest against mere outcries, to be led along by popular notions, popular sins, tendencies to evil which captivate the multitude—this is no part of a Christian clergyman's duty. He must surrender father and mother, wife and children, yea, and his own life also, if need be, to bear witness unto Him who said, "Woe unto you, when all men shall speak well of you!"

But not necessarily are the tendencies of the times wholly evil. They are often the yearnings of humanity after God. They are the blind gropings after that Invisible Master who "was lifted up from the earth to draw all men unto Him." The world of to-day is still on the whole a baptized world, pervaded by the spirit of Christianity. Its movements are not entirely evil. Nay, like all great moral movements, no matter what of ignorance, of folly, of wickedness there may be in them, no matter how often they need in part to be protested against, they have in them their own remedy. Used aright, passed through the crucible, tried like gold in the fire, brought to the foot of the Cross, tested by the faith once delivered to the saints, guided heavenward, they become tides in human affairs, which move toward that glorious day which is yet to dawn, when upon our astonished vision shall burst the "new heavens and the new earth, wherein dwelleth righteousness."

I do not, of course, mean to say that there are *not* in the world impulses wholly devil-born, tendencies to destruction and disintegration which we must fight to the death. But the insight which shall distinguish between these and those, which shall be able in the former case to discern between good and evil, to find the remedy in the tendency itself, by developing what is good and true in the movement, to overpower what is base and false—this in the State is Christian statesmanship; this in the Church is the "knowing what Israel ought to do," and is that blessed wisdom which will make the Christian minister "a man of understanding of the times."

Let me dwell then for a moment upon a marked tendency of the times. Men do not regard authority as they once did. To say that the fathers taught it, or the Church proclaims it, or that it has been held from immemorial time, or even that the Holy Scriptures assert it, does not command the unwavering assent of those who hear, as once it did. Men wish to learn the reasons of things. It is not enough to know that men in bygone generations have been satisfied; we must be satisfied also. In proportion as men are able to investigate, they search in every direction. They test Scripture by science. They find out the laws by which things are governed, and invade what once was deemed to be the realm of the supernatural, and show that the miracles of one age are sometimes the science of another. They pierce the bosom of the earth, and bring the hidden treasures of darkness to overthrow ancient traditions as to the age of the world and the antiquity of man. They trace history to its source and language to its primal roots. From Egyptian pyramids and Assyrian mounds they bring forth ancient inscriptions to confirm or contradict the sacred story. Each animal that moves, each plant that grows, each living thing, no matter what the order to which it belongs, is searched to bear its witness to the truth. Nay, they stand face to face with life itself, and dare to ask that impalpable, mysterious thing whether it comes from the Eternal God, or springs into existence by spontaneous power. Through all the region of created things, from stars that move in their courses down to the tiniest flower that blooms, they cry to all the visible and temporal, "Speak to us of God!" Nay, they search into man himself, and strive to understand the laws of his being, and the working of his will, and the deep recesses of that hidden spirit which makes him most like unto God. They cry unto their souls, and say, "In thy weakness and feebleness, in thy strength and majesty, in the shortness of time and the sorrows of humanity, tell me, O my spirit, has God revealed Himself to thee, and doest thou know that thou shalt never die?" O awful questionings of this day of ours! O pleading cries that go to Heaven from an unsettled world! To hear them aright is to be "a man of understanding of the times."

I am well aware that there are those who go far beyond such questions as those I have mentioned. I know that there are those who, whether from moral guilt or intellectual pride, pass beyond the proper bounds of reasonable inquiry, and the due search into truth, and, rearing their Babel-towers to heaven, proclaim another religion than the eternal truth of God.

Reason bears a threefold office toward revealed truth, and within that province is indeed supreme, but only there.

1. It is the province of Reason to state in terms that the understanding can apprehend what the truths are which Revelation has declared.

2. It is the province of Reason to state as clearly what revealed truth is *not*; for, while the Revelation of God is above and beyond Reason, it never can be contrary to it.

3. It is the province of Reason to investigate and test, by every process which the mind of man can conceive, the testimony which is borne to the truth of Revelation. The more it tests this testimony, whether it be by scientific research, or archaeological investigation, or the study of the mind of man, the more will that testimony stand forth sure and unshaken, the foundation of God, the same yesterday, to-day, and for ever!

But to go beyond the threefold office of the reason, and sit as a judge of revealed truth, and dare to say that this or that is untrue because it does not commend itself to the finite judgment—this is that very folly of which the Psalmist writes when he says, "The fool hath said in his heart, There is no God."

Of course, I must not be misunderstood as undervaluing the power of authority. Most men were not intended to be independent investigators of the truth of religion, but to receive it from others. I suppose the family and the Church were mercifully established, to send down from age to age the truth of God to children and to child-like hearts. Life is too short, and its duties are too many, for men to be laying over and over again the very foundations of religion. There is a great deal of unreality in some of the doubt of the time. There are people calling themselves skeptical, who only differ from Christians in having taken for their authoritative teacher some newspaper or review, some man of science, or modern philosopher, or popular preacher, instead of the grand old creeds, and the truths for which martyrs have died, and the unshaken faith of the Catholic Church. They are as much submitting to authority as the little child, only to authority not as reliable.

But I pass to another note of the times, and weave it with what I have already said, because the answer the minister of God must give to both is one and the same.

More people, in this western land, are led away from God by a sort of every-day materialism than by scientific doubt. They are practical men and women. They get lead and copper from the mines of Lake Superior, or gold and silver from California and Arizona. They plant huge farms upon the wide prairie-land, and bring to market innumerable bushels of corn. They hold real estate until either taxes ruin them or great cities make them rich. They build railroads, they deal in money and in stocks. Even if their work be professional, it is all directed to the furtherance of material ends, manufactures and commerce, trade and merchandise. Nor is this so with the rich and successful only: the pursuit of the food and raiment wherewith a man ought to be content— and rarely is—is just as eager and soul-engrossing. I do not for a moment mean to undervalue honest, faithful, hearty labor of any sort. To subdue and replenish the earth, to make the best and the most of what God has given us, is well. Only, too often, there lies underneath it the acceptance of the real and tangible, the things the body craves, the ear hears and the eye sees, instead of the invisible and unearthly. It is the utter absorption of the whole being, with all its powers and faculties, in what every one confesses is fleeting and temporal.

Is it a wonder that religion itself should be permeated by this
lurking materialism? The soul, engrossed in earthly pursuits, scouts
all mysteries. It wants its religion to be as practical as its business.
A comfortable church, where people may be able to listen pleas-
antly or doze easily; music that shall gratify the ear; preaching
that shall please the mind, and not too unpleasantly trouble the
conscience; pleasant talks on current events, nice discussions of
literary topics, clever dissertations on moral subjects; a minister
hired and well paid because his abilities deserve it, with the honest
determination to break the contract when his voice fails or age
enfeebles: this is no unfair picture.

On the other hand, a priesthood endowed by God with the
blessed commission to bind and to loose; sacraments capable of
carrying grace; the mighty power of prayer; the invisible ministra-
tions of the angels; the mystery of the Eternal Trinity; the glory of
the Incarnate Son; the Cross of Christ with its heights and depths,
with its story of sorrow, suffering, and shame; the deep burden of
sin; the awful powers of the world to come; the bands that bind
the living and the dead in one communion; the power, and
authority, and mission, and unity of the Church of God: all these
seem shadowy, and unreal, and unpractical. Yet still beyond these
voices stretches the invisible, spiritual world. The throne of God is
there. Around it is the rainbow, like unto an emerald; and before
it the unruffled peace of the crystal sea. With the voices of the four
and twenty elders, and the unnumbered hosts of angels and of men,
is blended the unceasing cry of the four living creatures, embody-
ing all created nature, saying: "Holy, holy, holy is the Lord God of
hosts." The ceaseless burden of prayer, the victories of faith, the
mysterious working of the sacraments, the wondrous conquests of
the Church of God, the upturned glances of little children, the
intercession of litanies, the sighs of penitents, the prayers of the
saints beneath the altar, are all borne into that mystic presence by
Him who is in the midst of the throne, the Lamb as it had been
slain. Let men reason as they will, let them grasp at what is earthly
and material as they may, the heavenly places still continue, and
men are set down in them in Christ Jesus.

And yet underneath both scientific doubt and ordinary materialism lies the same hidden cause. It is the realistic tendency of the

time, which clamors for facts, which seeks to grasp and realize and appropriate and understand all hidden truths, which will not rest until it has gone whithersoever human reason go, and found the laws which eternal wisdom has fashioned for the government of the world. This, which produces minute scientific investigation and philosophic study, gives to the practical man his active energy, his desire to conquer space and time with new devices of travel and communication. It is this which makes him seek to turn the hidden forces of nature, which seemed to be the very voice of God, into the obedient servant of the humblest man. It is this which makes him set even an undue value on money and food, and land and houses, and farm and merchandise, as if they were to last for ever; and while the passing years wail forth, "Earth to earth, dust to dust, ashes to ashes," answer back, "No particle of matter ever perishes; the energy that seems to vanish is only transferred; the force that disappears, appears again"; while coarser minds echo the old response, "Let us eat and drink, for to-morrow we die."

But if what we have stated be a tendency of the times, how shall the Israel of God and the minister of Christ gather healing from the poison and a remedy from the disease? Must it be by showing how scientific research is for ever answering its own doubts, and bearing witness to the truth it seemed to imperil? Must it be by showing how poor and little are the noblest results of man's labor, whether in the realm of thought or action, in the presence of sin, sorrow, and death? Must it be by calmly repeating the truth which never alters, the creeds which survive all changes, the faith once and for ever delivered to the saints? Must it be by clever arguments, in proof of sacramental grace, and the law of prayer, and the mysteries of religion, and the testimony of miracles and prophecy? All this is well; but there is something beyond these, which seems to be the very remedy which is the burden of the lesson I would teach to-day.

The answer to a realistic, practical, material age, by the Church and the ministry, is a realistic, practical, and in some sort material one; nor has the Church along the ages failed to give it. A life of supernatural self-denial on the part of her ministry; the surrender of home and friends, wife and children, money and lands; the burning love for the souls of men which is satisfied with nothing short of their salvation; the earnest, practical, faithful labor of the members of the Church; the watching night and day by the bedside of the suffering and the sick, the tender care for little children, the unfailing mercy which seeks for Christ's sheep scattered abroad, wherever they are; the hospital with the sisters of charity; the reformatory for the abandoned and lost; the church open all the day long for the passer-by to kneel and pray; the offered sacrifice of the Holy Communion in the early morning; louder than all arguments, better than any logic, these will convince a practical and material age of the truth of that supernatural world, of which the apostle declares that the things which are unseen are eternal.

Does any one doubt whether these are a sufficient answer? Does some one scornfully ask, "Is this all the reply the Church and its ministry can make to scientific research, or philosophic study, or the soul-engrossing love of material things?" I answer: In the face of two ever-present realities this response will be powerful beyond all human reckoning. These two realities are Sin and Death! What can science or philosophy or earthly possessions say to the soul weighed down with a sense of guilt—what can they cry to the sorrow-laden spirit as it stands beside the still cold form of father or mother, wife or child, or feels itself the icy touch of the King of Terrors? Then, O my friends, the Cross of Christ, the invisible world, the rest of heaven, the Communion of Saints, the work of the priesthood, the presence of Jesus—these, and these alone, can be the staff and the stay, the refuge and the rescue, of the soul of man!

But, O my brother, how mighty in your soul must be the grace of God, that you may be able to make this answer in this day of ours! There must be simple child-like faith which never hesitates or waivers, which is "the substance of things hoped for, the evidence of things not seen." There must be careful, earnest prayer, and the labor for that divine wisdom which is able to convince the gainsaying. There must be prudence and skill, and such a love for souls as will overpower, and subdue, and correct each fault and failing of the natural man. There must be utter self-surrender of the affections, mind, and will to Him who will accept no divided service. There must be, if you would do your work well, the clear understanding of that blessed sacramental system, by which it pleases God to regenerate and wash the sin-stained soul white in the blood of Jesus, and bring the forgiven penitent into the presence of the Invisible King.

Nor must you look for success and easy days. To him who would do his Master's work aright, there must be the crown of thorns, the Cross his Master bore. And does this seem too much to call you to, my son? Does the heart shrink and the eye fill with tears, with what, if you care not for the world, its honors, its applause, or its approval, is sure to come? Then, remember, there is no peace on earth like the peace of self-surrender; no happiness below like the happiness of self-denial; no love of father or mother, wife or children, like the love of the souls for whom the Master died. And, oh, so soon the days pass by and the years! Life is only a dream that for ever vanishes. Beyond are the only realities; there, and only there, is the true life of souls!

Whether it be sooner or later, it will be but a moment when the sunset gates shall unbar, and from the glorious city flash the eternal splendor. Forth shall the King in His beauty come, with all His shining train, and welcome you—if the work has been truly done—to the land where there is no more sorrow nor crying, the Peace of God for ever and ever!

THE MISSION OF THE CHURCH OF GOD

(Preached at Convocation in Milwaukee, April 19, 1876.)

> "Then contended I with the rulers, and said, Why is
> the House of God forsaken?"—Nehemiah xiii., 11.

To PROCLAIM THE gospel of Christ; to do His work upon earth; to be in His stead a messenger of love, mercy, and pardon to mankind; by the mighty power of the Holy Ghost; to make Christ present, though hidden from mortal gaze—this is the work of the Church of God.

A test of the Church's vigor in this respect is its power to propagate itself. If it lives it must grow; if it be Christ's Body it must be full of zeal for the souls for which He died. It must be true of her as it was of Him, that she has a work to do, and that she must be straitened until it is accomplished. She will not need to be preached to, and exhorted, and reasoned and pleaded with, any more than trees and plants and the mother earth, in the springtime, when the sun shines and the rain falls, have to be urged to put forth leaves and flowers. Her mission is to win souls, to convert, to baptize, to offer the mystical sacrifice, to absolve, to heal, to bind up the broken hearts, to bring again the outcast, to advance with unbroken front, to speak with an unfaltering voice, and to make the wilderness and solitary place to be glad for her, and the desert to rejoice and blossom as the rose. If she has this power, she lives; if not, in the words of the text, the house of God is indeed forsaken.

The speaker of the words of the text was a layman, a reformer, a helper of the Church, a man whose life was given up to God, an inspired teacher, and one who was an example of what all these should be; and when he found the house of God forsaken, he said unto the *rulers*, "Why is it so?"

I do not intend to prove this evening that the Church is not accomplishing its work, nor to bring statistics together to show that there is any decline in her influence. I do not know that it is so. I have no dismal forebodings to utter with regard to the future, for my heart is full of hope. The only point wherein the words of my text have any application is in the thought already indicated, that the house of God is forsaken if the Church does not do her missionary work with zeal, with earnestness, with a sort of generous prodigality, and with real success; and that if she does not do so it can not be her own fault, for she is the Bride of Christ, all glorious within, though the wrought gold of her clothing be dimmed and her raiment of needlework torn; but it is the fault of the rulers.

I have only one statistic to mention. The State of Wisconsin, comprising two Dioceses, consists of about fifty-four thousand square miles, with a population in 1870 of over one million of people; and the Church in the year 1874 had fewer than five thousand communicants. I am well aware of all the reasons for the smallness of the number of communicants, the great efforts of the various bodies of Christians who are earnestly laboring, the large foreign population, the many reasons which prevent conversions in great numbers. I am quite aware of the fact that we are better off than some other Western Dioceses. But with all these allowances the disproportion is a startling one, in view of the claims of the Church, and of the blessings which it is hers to proclaim.

If I go on to assert that the disproportion is the fault of the Church's rulers, I hope I shall not be misunderstood to mean this or that person or body of persons, parishes, Council, Standing Committee, priests, bishops. No one, I think, can watch the labor of most of our clergy and of the various committees appointed to work, without finding great toil, earnest zeal, and, I must say, results *not* in proportion to either.

If the fault be anywhere, it must lie, over and above whatever want of zeal there is in the most zealous of us, in our methods of work and in the organization that governs and controls us. The work we have to do; the burden that is laid upon each one of God's priests, ay, and on the lay members of the Church also; the awful answer we must one day give; the need, the crying need everywhere must be—not my excuse, for none is needed—but the motive which makes it right to speak of what may be the difficulties we ought to remove.

The first point to which I desire to call your attention is that the distinctive doctrines of the Church are not as definitely and positively proclaimed as they ought to be. Between the Roman Church on the one hand, which declares herself to be the one Catholic Church of Christ, to the exclusion of all others, and the various orthodox and unorthodox denominations which claim to preach Christ to the world, I do not know what reason our Church has to exist, except it be, on the one hand, that she is the American branch of the Catholic Church, and on the other that, because she is so, she can do what no other Christian body can accomplish. That she is a conservative, respectable, highly cultivated, refined body of people, that she has a Scriptural liturgy and even a sound body of doctrine, will hardly prove a sufficient reason for being merely another of the great number of denominations which do the work of Christ, or seek to do it, with all the weakness of disunion, divided counsels, and separate and opposing organizations.

The Church of which we are the priests and members puts forth definite claims to do, by an Apostolic Ministry, what God has bidden the Church to do. These are to administer the sacraments— sacraments which profess to be a reality: a Baptism which regenerates, a Holy Eucharist which gives the threefold blessing of the presence of Christ by means of the sacramental presence of His human nature, of the pleading of the one sacrifice once offered by virtue of that presence, and of union with Christ resulting therefrom to the penitent believer; to train up children with true Christian training; to preach the Gospel to sinners, and to have power to bind and to loose, in the name of God and by His commission, the sin-stricken soul; in an age of materialsim to present the supernatural world, with all its hidden powers, to the acceptance of mankind; to preach chastity, honor, honesty, family life, and patriotic earnestness to the people; to visit the sick, to clothe the naked, to comfort prisoners, to soothe the dying, and to bear witness to the invisible bonds which bind the living and the dead in one Communion.

These are distinctive claims. If they are false, no priest should dare to present them. If they are true, the Church must dare to proclaim and to practice them. No questions of caution, or prudence, or the fear of offending, can possibly come in, in such questions as these. If it is the Church's mission to do all this, she needs to do it; and the more directly, plainly, without reserve, she does it, the more likely it is that she will accomplish her work.

But—and here is the point—all this needs to be done, not so much by individual effort and individual courage, though these are necessary, as by the organized system of the Church.

Let me suggest some points which do not seem to tend in this direction.

First: Every devout American Churchman believes in the due influence of the laity of the Church in her government, but they ought to be laymen. A layman, I suppose, is a baptized member of the Church who desires to any degree to exercise his privileges as such. I give the feeblest definition I can give, saying nothing about the reception of the Holy Communion and many other duties of Christians. By the laws which govern the Church in Wisconsin, and I believe generally in this country, any person, baptized or unbaptized, who has for six months attended its services, and statedly contributes to the support of an Episcopal Parish, can exercise the duties of a layman in that parish. He can vote for the vestry; he can have his share in electing the lay delegates to the Council; he can thus have a vote and voice, through his representative, in the election of a parish priest, in the general government of the parish, in the legislation of the Diocese, in the election of a Bishop, in the election of delegates to the General Convention, and in the power, therefore, to alter the Prayer Book and to govern the American branch of the Church of Christ.

All these powers the lay members of the Church ought to have; but nothing but Baptism can make a man a lay member. Money, instead of grace, the power to contribute to the support of a parish, is made the basis of representation, instead of that initiatory sacrament without which a man can not bear even the name of Christian. This, of course, is no question as to whether women shall have the right to vote in parishes; it is not a question whether members of a vestry or of the Diocesan Council ought to be communicants; it lies down at the very root of our organized life, and needs to be extirpated.

That it does not produce such bad results as one might anticipate is due to two limiting circumstances: first, that the larger number of persons who vote in parishes consists of baptized persons; and secondly, that the persons voted for are generally required to be either communicants or at least baptized, though this is not the invariable rule. But, while this is so, who can estimate the deadly evil which must work like a poison through our whole organization, that the qualification for exercising the duty and right of a lay member of the Church should be a money qualifi-cation? What lurking Erastianism, what love of the world, what lack of faith there must be, that this can be, and that year after year it goes on, and the Christian consciousness of the Church does not rise against it.

I pass over the various evils which are the results of this primary evil—the tendency to make the clergy hirelings; the false constitu-tion and character thereby given to parishes; the steady lowering of the ministerial character which it has the tendency to promote—because my object is to mention another great difficulty in our organization, which has no doubt a kindred root with that already mentioned.

Theoretically, the well-trained Churchman has a very lofty idea of the Episcopal office—sometimes an exaggerated notion of it; and yet while this exists, practically the office is shorn of its real glory. The money-qualified electors choose the Vestry and the delegates to the Council; the lay delegates have either an actual, or, at any rate, a veto power in the election of a Bishop. It is not surprising that they should feel as if the elected Bishop had simply such powers as may be conferred upon him by the Constitution and Canons of the Church, which they or their predecessors have formed, and which at any time may, by due form of law, be altered. Hence, a Bishop's work and duty is whatever the Canons require him to do. He is to ordain, and confirm, and hold visita-tions; he is to preside at councils and be the chairman of commit-tees. He is to be the pleasant guest of the chief layman of the parish and advise the clergyman when advice is needed. He is to attend to routine duties without end, and, above all, to be in journeyings often. If he can preach well and talk well; if he is provident and cautious and a good executive officer; if he has personal influence and an untiring physique; if his digestion is unimpaired, his nerves unruffled; if he concentrates himself upon nothing, and diffuses a mild Episcopal perfume over everything, he meets the common theory which prevails of what a Bishop ought to be.

The opposite theory only needs to be stated. He receives the Holy Ghost for the office and work of a Bishop in the Church of God. He is bound to be an overseer, to confirm, to ordain, to do all the works I have mentioned. But, above all, he is called to be one upon whose soul the awful burden is laid to convert men to the obedience of the faith. He must offer the Holy Eucharist; he must preach the Word; he must bind and loose; he must organize; he must, above all things, be a shepherd, a guide, a Father. The Canons of the Church are simply the directions according to which he exercises his office. Wheresoever they do not limit that office, the inherent powers remain; and to convert men to Christ, to be the chief pastor of his Diocese—this is the Bishop's glory.

Hence the "see system," as it is called; which simply means that the Bishop who would thus exercise his office must needs do it within definite limits of space, and where the want is greatest, that is, where life and population have met together, in the city, rather than primarily over long lines of railways and interminable prairies.

Hence, too, the need of the Bishop's Church, and the Chapter of devout and earnest clergy, to be the central expressions of his work and power—the heart whence life flows forth to all the members, and which, while it makes his work more effective, gives the true constitutional check upon any possibility of despotism. Placed in this position at the center of his work, surrounded and upheld by devout, dignified, and independent priests, counseled and supported by faithful and educated laymen, the Bishop can become, as he never can in any other way, the true missionary of his Diocese.

Two things will largely contribute to this result. The Bishop's Chapter must be a missionary body. In it will be the officers of the Diocese, who have in charge the financial, missionary, and

educational works of the Diocese. When, then, the Bishop goes
forth to care for any need of his people, to visit, to preach, to
revive the work, to seek for Christ's sheep that are scattered abroad,
he does so with the knowledge of the whole position, with the aid
of those who are caring for the needs in question, with a power
which does not belong to one man, however great those powers
may possibly be, but with the combined wisdom, fervor, and
power of the very heart and center of his Diocese. The second
thing is that, wherever he plants missions, the "see" idea will be
the model after which he establishes them. The common way in
which missionaries are sent does not tend to true and orderly
growth, and is injurious to ministerial efficiency. There comes a
request from some small village, or town or country neighborhood,
for a clergyman. It is backed by some effort on the part of a
faithful few. A rich man or so, who thinks that an Episcopal
Church will assist the growing community, promises a contribution
or gives it, and becomes thereby the chief layman of the parish. A
small missionary stipend is added, and the clergyman is sent. Away
from his brethren, struggling to maintain a family with insufficient
means, without books, drawing an occasional stimulus from the
visit of the Bishop, a convocation, or a convention, what wonder
if he goes from place to place, and loses heart and vigor, and can
not grow! And then the interminable evils of half-organized,
imperfectly constituted parishes, the gossip and quarreling, the
ignorance and conceit, until what was meant to be for the salvation
of souls fails of its full power and effect.

Suppose, on the other hand, a body of clergy, four or five, under
the guidance of some well-trained priest in a large town, with due
subordination and guarded rights, a Chapter like that at the
Cathedral, and, like it, under the Bishop. The most effective work,
orderly services, the teaching of the young, the care of public
institutions—all these could be done by such a body; and, in
addition, missionary stations within a radius of thirty miles could
be served by them far more usefully than if the clergyman resided
in the smaller community. If the Cathedral Chapter and some of
the smaller chapters in the other cities included in the staff of
clergy an itinerant missionary, who had his headquarters in the

city, and went forth, under guidance, wherever even a solitary family of Churchmen might be—baptizing, administering the Communion, preaching and visiting—it might come to pass, and would, that there need not be in the Diocese a single Church family anywhere that would not be under the care of the Church, its Mother.

Such a system as this proposed would meet, I believe, another question which is of the gravest importance in all missionary efforts—the proper way to raise money. There are but two things necessary to get all the money that is needed for Christian work, and more than is wanted: Faith in the things for which money is asked, and the application to and the request of every human being who calls himself a lay member of the Church, to give. Great sums are not obtained by large donations; they come from many small gifts, and the amount of many small gifts is spiritually a million-fold greater than the same amount given by two or three. A system that will meet all the people with the Saviour's words, "It is more blessed to give than to receive," will never have a deficient treasury. Believe it, my brethren, concentration, a true Episcopal work, the defense of the rights of laymen and laywomen against mere money, will produce a missionary system which will cement, renew, and strengthen, and make the Church go forth, upon her heaven-commanded mission, "fair as the moon, clear as the sun, and terrible as an army with banners."

Nor will it do to speak of this system as a dream, as the proposal of enthusiasm, as the visions of youth, or with any of the other epithets with which those whose enthusiasm is dead seek to destroy the efforts of the earnest. The system has this great claim upon the attention of Churchmen, that it is the Catholic system which, whensoever it has been adhered to, has won the greatest victories for the Faith, and wheresoever it has been departed from, has been the cause of disaster and pitiable failure.

Nor is one as likely to hear, to-day, the old objection, that the Episcopal system is so exactly modeled after the government of the country, that to depart from it is, in some sort, to lack in patriotism. One's lips are almost closed when this objection is used, lest there should be too much said or too little. But is not this beginning to be felt by the thoughtful—nay, is it not ready to burst

from the hearts of thousands—that we are not living in the republic
of our forefathers? Is not the time at hand when the educated and
the thoughtful, when the religious and the true of all denominations and bodies of believers, will demand a conservative, high-
minded, Christian government—a true, earnest, free and constitutional republic?

The evils in the Church are not the same as in the country, but
they have, no doubt, arisen from a reversal of the true idea of all
Church government—namely, that power, like grace, descends
from above, not from below. From the apostles to the elders and
brethren, from the apostles to their successors in every age, from
the days when the risen Saviour breathed on them and said, "Receive ye the Holy Ghost," to our own time, from the bishops to
the priests, from the Church to her children everywhere, and from
Christ, who has said, "Lo, I am with you always, unto the end of
the world," the benediction descends. For when He ascended up
on high, we read that He gave His gifts unto men; and what were
these gifts? "He gave some apostles, and some prophets, and some
evangelists, and some pastors and teachers, for the perfecting of
the saints, for the work of the ministry, for the edifying of the
body of Christ, until we all come, in the unity of the spirit and the
bond of peace, unto the measure of the stature of the fullness of
Christ."

Brethren, let us seek to believe and to dare; let us cast away
dependence on riches and fashion and worldly opinion; let us
preach the Gospel to the poor; let us surrender all things to Christ;
let us organize our work after the fashion of catholic order and
primitive precedent, and leave the rest. Christ is our refuge and
strength; Christ is our Leader and Guide; Christ is our Bishop and
Pastor; and, if the ship of the Church be tossed on stormy waves
by rudest blasts, then will He come walking upon the waters, and
say, "Peace, be still!"

Or, if for us is meant to be the day dark and gloomy, and the
heavens black with clouds and abundance of rain, it matters not.
On the shore of the everlasting morning, still our Lord is waiting,
it may be for others to drag the net to shore full of great fishes;
one hundred and fifty and three; yet with His loving welcome will
He receive us, who have fed, however unworthily, His sheep and
His lambs.